Mars

by Steven L. Kipp

Content Consultants:
Rod Nerdahl
Program Director, Minneapolis Planetarium

Diane Kane
Space Center Houston

Bridgestone Books
an imprint of Capstone Press

Bridgestone Books are published by Capstone Press
818 North Willow Street, Mankato, Minnesota 56001
http://www.capstone-press.com

Library of Congress Cataloging-in-Publication Data
Kipp, Steven L.
    Mars/Steven L. Kipp.
    p. cm.--(The galaxy)
    Summary: Discusses the surface features, atmosphere, exploration,
and other aspects of the planet Mars.
    ISBN 1-56065-607-7
    1. Mars (Planet)--Juvenile literature. [1. Mars (Planet)]
I. Title. II. Series: Kipp, Steven L.   Galaxy.
QB641.K35   1998
523.43--dc21

                                                        97-6922
                                                          CIP
                                                           AC

Photo credits
NASA, cover, 6, 8, 10, 12, 14, 16, 18, 20

Table of Contents

The Solar System and Mars 5
The Planet Mars 7
Canals 9
Spaceprobes 11
More Discoveries 13
Atmosphere 15
On Mars 17
Rotation and Revolution 19
Moons 21

Hands On: Make Martian Sand 22
Words to Know 23
Read More 23
Useful Addresses 24
Internet Sites 24
Index 24

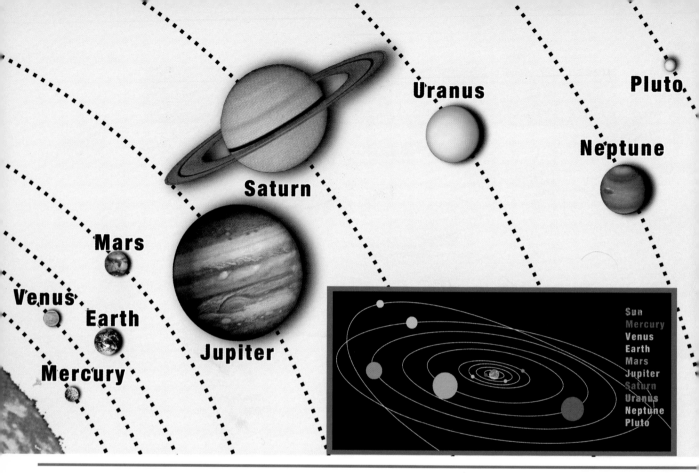

Saturn

Uranus

Pluto

Neptune

Mars

Jupiter

Venus

Earth

Mercury

Sun
Mercury
Venus
Earth
Mars
Jupiter
Saturn
Uranus
Neptune
Pluto

Planet Facts

Mars

Diameter–4,217 miles (6,786 kilometers)

Distance from Sun–142 million miles (227 million kilometers)

Moons–Two

Revolution Period–687 days

Rotation Period–24 and one-half hours

Earth

Diameter–7,927 miles (12,756 kilometers)

Distance from Sun–93 million miles (150 million kilometers)

Moons–One

Revolution Period–365 days

Rotation Period–23 hours and 56 minutes

The Solar System and Mars

Mars is part of the solar system. This includes the Sun, planets, and objects traveling with them. The solar system is always moving.

The Sun is the center of the solar system. Everything in the solar system circles around the Sun. The Sun is a star. A star is a ball of very hot gases. Stars like the Sun give off heat and light.

There are nine known planets in the solar system. Planets are the nine heavenly bodies that circle the Sun. Mars is one of them.

Mars is the fourth planet away from the Sun. It is about 142 million miles (227 million kilometers) away from the Sun. Mars circles around the Sun at the speed of 60,400 miles (97,200 kilometers) per hour. Mars also rotates as it travels. This means it spins.

Many people think that there could have been life on Mars. So far, scientists have not found any living things.

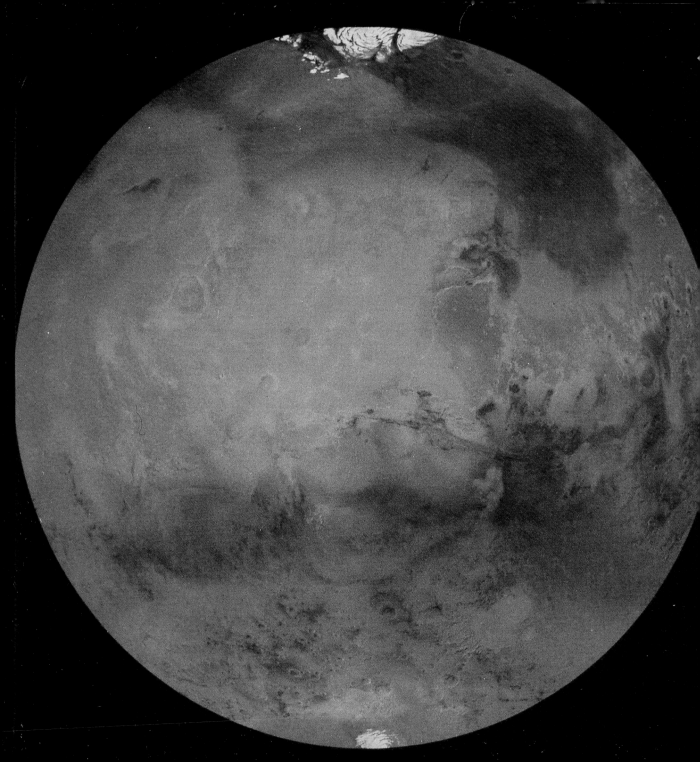

The Planet Mars

Mars is smaller than Earth. It is only 4,218 miles (6,749 kilometers) wide. Seven planets the size of Mars could fit into one Earth.

People can easily see Mars in the night sky. This is because Mars is close to Earth. Only the planets Venus and Mercury come closer to Earth.

Early Italians looked at Mars with a telescope. A telescope makes faraway objects look larger and closer. They saw that Mars has an orange-red color. This made them think of blood. They named the planet Mars after their god of war.

Early scientists called astronomers studied Mars. Astronomy is the study of stars, planets, and space. Astronomers did not understand Mars.

Some astronomers thought there were aliens on Mars. Aliens are creatures from another planet. They called the aliens Martians. Writers wrote popular stories and movies about Martians.

Mars' orange-red color reminded early Italians of blood.

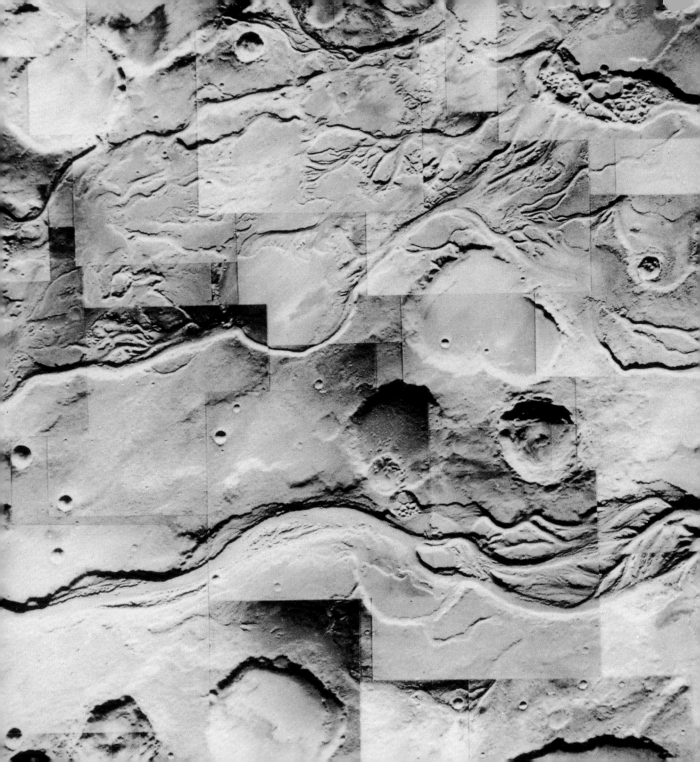

Canals

In the 1800s, an astronomer named Giovanni Schiaparelli studied Mars. Schiaparelli looked at Mars with his telescope.

Schiaparelli thought he saw lines on Mars. He called these lines canali. This Italian word can mean river channels or canals made by people. River channels are thin streams of water. Nature makes river channels. Canals are thin lines of water like river channels. But people dig canals through land.

Schiaparelli really meant river channels. But people misunderstood. They thought he meant canals made by people. They felt that Martians must have built the canals.

The U.S. astronomer Percival Lowell also studied Mars in the 1800s. He told people that he saw canals, too. Lowell believed that Martians had dug the canals. He thought the canals brought water that helped Martians farm.

Schiaparelli thought he saw these river channels on Mars.

Spaceprobes

Scientists cannot see Mars clearly from Earth. So scientists made spaceprobes. A spaceprobe is a special type of aircraft built to visit outer space. Outer space is space outside of a planet's atmosphere. An atmosphere is the mix of gases that surrounds some planets.

Scientists sent Mariner and Viking spaceprobes to Mars. These spaceprobes helped scientists learn more about Mars.

The spaceprobes took pictures of Mars. These pictures showed that craters cover parts of Mars. Craters are large holes in the ground. Meteorites from outer space crashed into Mars and made the craters. Meteorites are big pieces of rock.

The spaceprobes also showed that the atmosphere of Mars is very thin. Living things need a certain kind of atmosphere to live. Scientists did not find living things on Mars.

Spaceprobes took pictures of Mars.

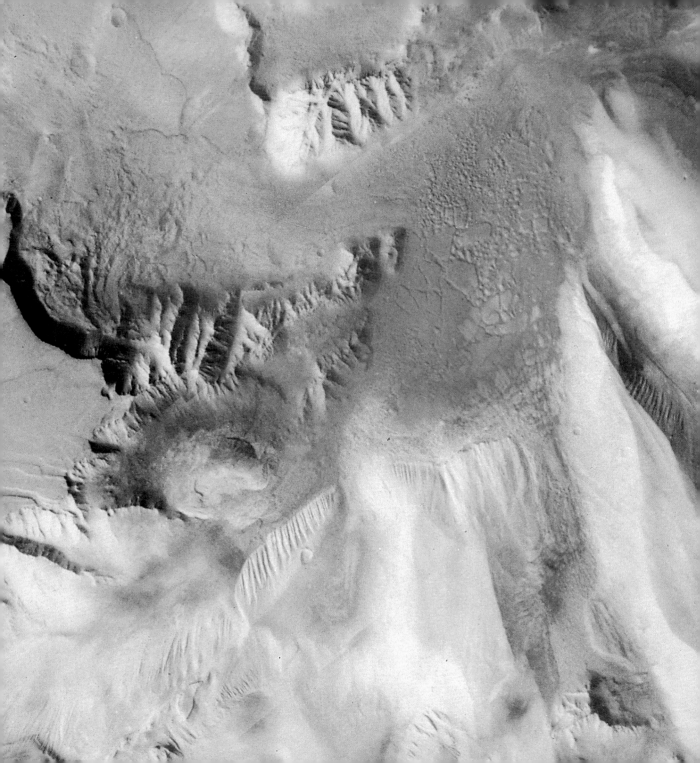

More Discoveries

In 1972, the Mariner 9 spaceprobe went into orbit around Mars. Orbit means to circle around another object. Mariner 9 was the first spaceprobe to orbit another planet.

Mariner 9 made many discoveries. It found a huge canyon system on Mars. A canyon is a deep area with steep sides.

Mariner 9 also found the solar system's largest known volcano on Mars. A volcano is a mountain that forms over a hole in a planet's crust. Crust is the outermost part of a planet. Sometimes volcanoes erupt. This happens when melted rock called lava flows out of their holes.

Mariner 9 also discovered that Mars has dry river channels. Once, water flowed in these channels. The channels that Mariner 9 found cannot be seen from Earth. Schiaparelli and Lowell did not see these channels.

Mariner 9 found a huge canyon system on Mars.

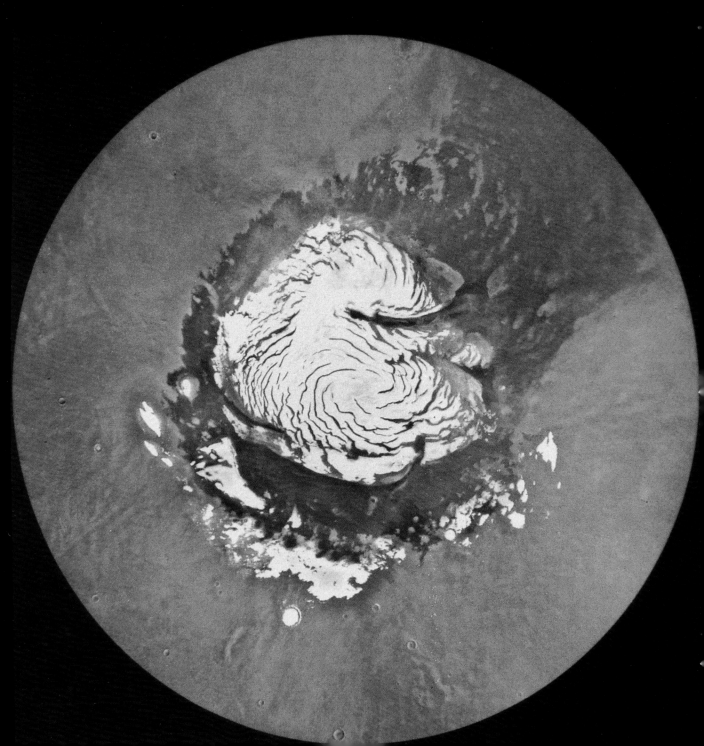

Atmosphere

Mars does not have much atmosphere because of its gravity. Gravity is a force that pulls things down. It keeps things from floating away into space. The gravity of Mars is too weak to keep gases around it. Most gases float into outer space.

The atmosphere on Mars has many gases. It is mostly made of carbon dioxide gas. Humans could not breathe on Mars. Humans need to breathe in oxygen.

A planet's atmosphere helps it hold in heat from the Sun. Because Mars has so little atmosphere, it becomes cold. The heat escapes into outer space. It becomes so cold that the carbon dioxide gas freezes. This makes carbon dioxide ice on the ground.

All of the water on Mars is frozen, too. Most of the ice is at Mars' most northern and southern parts. Some ice melts during summer on Mars. The ice freezes again during winter.

Mars has ice at its most northern and southern parts.

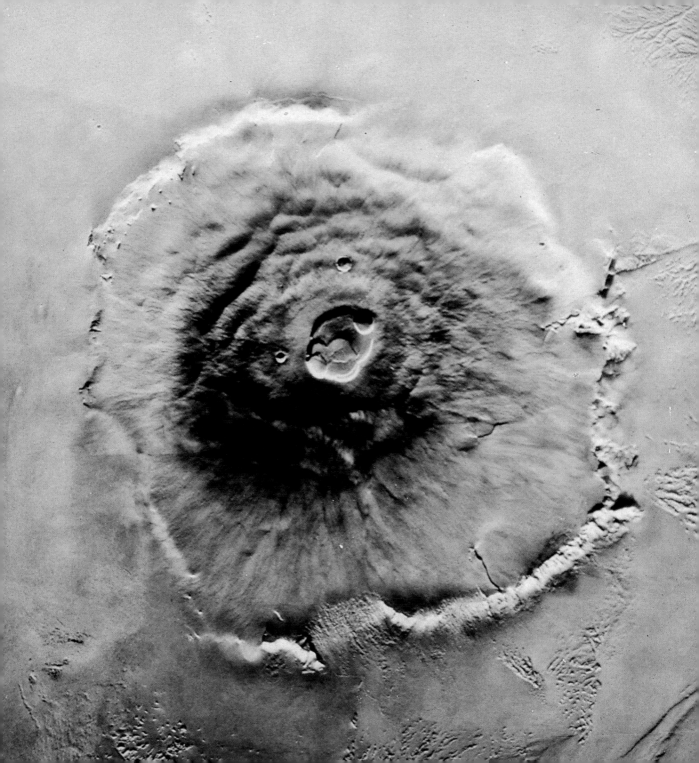

Some areas of Mars look like land on Earth. The northern part of Mars has many volcanoes. Flat plains are in between the volcanoes. The plains were formed by lava. Other parts of Mars are covered with craters, sand, and small rocks.

The sand and small rocks have a mix of iron and oxygen. Iron is a metal, and oxygen is a gas. The two items mix together and make iron oxide. Iron oxide is also known as rust. Iron oxide makes the sand and rocks on Mars orange-red. The winds on Mars blow the sand around.

The Tharsis Bulge is near the middle of Mars. There, four huge volcanoes rise above the land. Olympus Mons is the tallest and largest known volcano in our solar system. It is the size of the U.S. state of Missouri. The giant Mariner Valley is also near the Tharsis Bulge. Mariner Valley is a crack in the crust of Mars. It is more than 3,000 miles (4,800 kilometers) long.

Olympic Mons is the size of the U.S. state of Missouri.

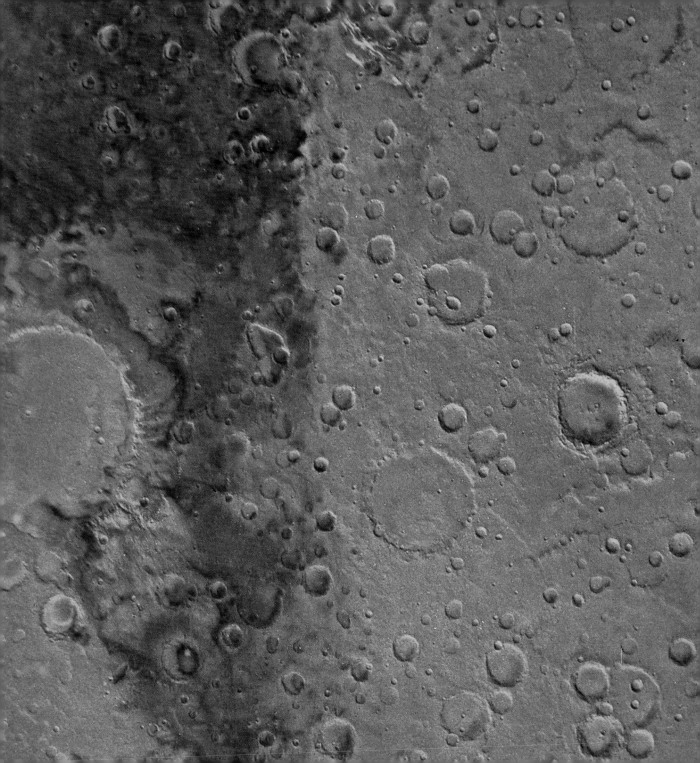

Rotation and Revolution

Mars spins as it moves through space. One complete spin is called a rotation. This is the length of a planet's day. It takes Mars 24 and one-half hours to spin around once. Earth spins around once about every 24 hours. The length of a day on Earth and on Mars is almost the same.

Scientists measure rotation time by finding a planet's large surface feature. They measure the time and place they first see the feature. The feature revolves with the planet. Scientists measure the time the feature takes to complete an entire circle. This gives them the rotation time.

Mars orbits the Sun like Earth does. Orbit means to circle around an object. One complete circle around the Sun is called a revolution. One revolution is equal to a planet's year. It takes Mars 687 Earth days to circle the Sun. This makes a year on Mars almost twice as long as an Earth year.

Scientists find a large surface feature to measure rotation time.

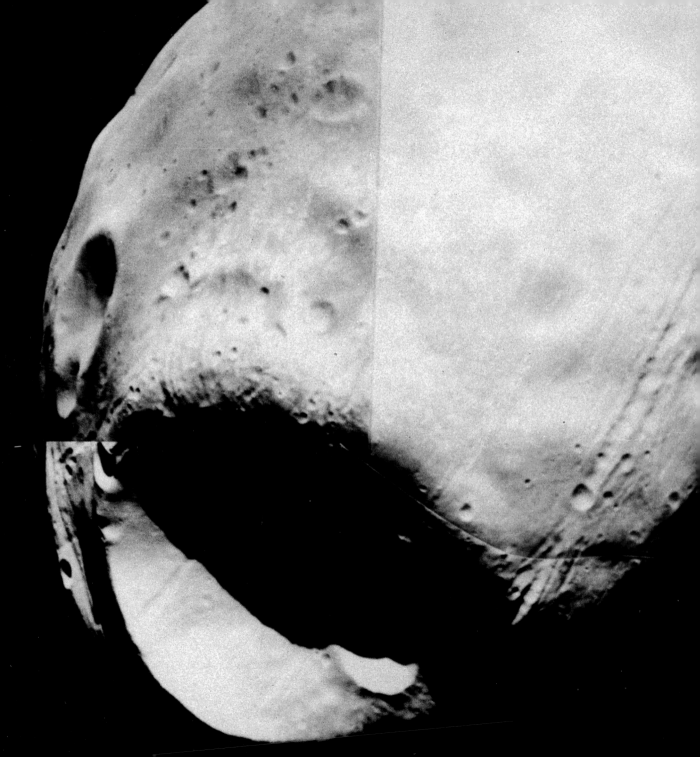

Moons

Mars has two moons that circle it. A scientist named the moons Phobos and Deimos. Phobos and Deimos are the sons of an early Italian god of war.

Phobos is Mars' largest moon. It is 17 miles (27 kilometers) wide. It orbits at just 3,000 miles (4,800 kilometers) above the surface of Mars.

Deimos is only nine miles (14 kilometers) wide. It orbits at more than 12,500 miles (20,000 kilometers) above the surface of Mars.

Scientists are always learning new things about Mars. Today's scientists think they have discovered signs of past Martian life. They still need to answer more questions to be sure.

Scientists are sending new spaceprobes to Mars. The spaceprobes will map the surface of Mars. Scientists also hope that the spaceprobes will find more answers. The new information may show if there once was life on Mars.

Phobos is Mars' largest moon.

Hands On: Make Martian Sand

The dust on Mars is orange-red. This is because of iron oxide. Iron oxide is also known as rust. You can see rust on cars. You can make your own Martian sand.

What You Need
Three large pieces of steel wool
Scissors
A pie plate
Sand
Water

What You Do
1. Cut the steel wool into small pieces.
2. Fill your pie plate half full with sand.
3. Mix the small pieces of steel wool in with the sand.
4. Mix one cup of water with the sand and steel wool.

In a couple of days, your sand will look orange-red. The iron oxide mixed with the sand like it did on Mars. You now have your own Martian sand.

Words to Know

astronomy (uh-STRON-uh-mee)—the study of stars, planets, and space

atmosphere (AT-muhss-fihr)—the mix of gases that surrounds some planets

crater (KRAY-tur)—a hole made when large pieces of rock crash into a planet or moon's surface

meteorite (MEE-tee-ur-rite)—a big piece of rock from outer space

revolution (rev-uh-LOO-shuhn)—one body circling another like planets circle the Sun

rotation (roh-TAY-shuhn)—to spin around

Read More

Brankley, Franklyn. *The Planets in Our Solar System.* New York: Harper & Row, 1981.

Seymour, Simon. *Mars*. New York: William Morrow and Company, 1987.

Vogt, Gregory. *Mars and the Inner Planets*. New York: Franklin Watts, 1982.

Useful Addresses

NASA Headquarters
300 E Street SW
Washington, DC 20546

National Air & Space Museum
Smithsonian Institution
Washington, DC 20560

Internet Sites

Kids Web—Astronomy and Space
http://www.npac.syr.edu/textbook/kidsweb/astronomy.html

NASA Homepage
http://www.nasa.gov/NASA_homepage.html

StarChild: A Learning Center for Young Astronomers
http://heasarc.gsfc.nasa.gov/docs/StarChild/StarChild.html

Index

astronomy, 7
atmosphere, 11, 15
Deimos, 21
gravity, 15
Lowell, Percival, 9, 13
Mariner Valley, 17
martian, 7, 21
meteorite, 11

Olympus Mons, 17
Phobos, 21
Schiaparelli, Giovanni, 9, 13
solar system, 5
spaceprobe, 11, 13, 21
star, 5
Sun, 5, 15, 19
volcano, 13, 17